30 Days
to a
Mindful Home

by Kathy Walsh

joyohboy
raising peaceful kids

thanks

My daughters Kara Walsh and Kayle Hope
for all the lessons you taught me

Annie Yonkers ~ book design

Kristin Bundesen ~ moral support

Trip Rothschild ~ love

Meredith Astles ~ marketing and partnership skills

Published by Joy Oh Boy Books
www.joyohboy.com

introduction

A mindful home…I wonder what that is.

When people think of a mindful home they imagine a home that is dripping with Buddhas while everything is Feng Shui perfect. In a mindful home people meditate an hour every day, have no judgment of others, always live in the moment, and experience peace & calm. "Bah Humbug" I say! This is not real. In real life things happen; it is how we deal with them that counts. Life is like a river - if we resist the flow it becomes hard. If we go with the flow and experience feelings like hurt and happiness along the way, we can truly live a life of **joy**. Incorporating a few mindful activities every day consistently will go a long way to create a peaceful family. Similar to a diet and exercise programs, extreme methods rarely work long term. This book, **30 Days to a Mindful Home**, is designed to give you some ideas to try out, as well as fun and mindful steps to incorporate into your daily routine. Along the way, some will stick and resonate with you more than others. I invite you to try them, reflect on what works for you and why and at the end of thirty days decide what to incorporate in your home on a regular basis. Have fun!

Let's get started!

intention

Intention is a powerful force that sets everything in motion. Many people never even think about an intention for their home and yet, it is the foundation. What is your intention for your home? Have you thought about it? Fill in the blank: in this home we... are compassionate to animals, grateful for nature, kind, positive, non-judgmental...whatever is important to you.

For me it was always important to listen to our own hearts and let our intuition guide us. I always believed that we have all the answers inside of us. So that was first on my list. In this home we ask our heart a question and let our own heart guide us.

Being kind to animals is another biggie for me. I love animals and feel deeply connected to them. A home that is kind and loving to pets sets a tone of love that permeates throughout the entire home.

Being allowed to express feelings was also important to me. I was lucky to grow up with a mother who projected happiness all the time. Although that was wonderful to be around, there was no space to be mad, frustrated or hurt. It was important to me that we had the space in my home to express negative feelings as well as positive.

A mindful home is not a perfect home, but it is a home that sees the good in everything and everyone. It's a home that focuses on the positive, lives in the moment, appreciates nature and animals and has an attitude of gratitude. So think about your intention, then write it down, frame it and hang it where everyone can see it. Words are powerful and intention is everything. Without it there is no direction, it's like driving a car without a steering wheel. So the very first order of business in having a mindful home is **intention**.

What is your intention to create a mindful home?

_____

_____

_____

_____

_____

_____

_____

_____

_____

_____

_____

_____

_____

_____

planning

I put this second because, like intention, it also sets the day for the household in motion. If you wanted to lose weight you would have a plan, correct? I am going to eat five small meals a day... I will avoid restaurants... I commit to half an hour of walking every day... Whatever the plan is, you would have to have it or you would end up starving and eating some garbage snack because you never planned for the day or the week.

It's the same thing with a mindful home. Think about the week ahead. What is the rhythm to the week? Will you have tech-free time? Will you have nature time? If the week is intense, will you balance it with some peaceful time?

I remember always being so excited about summer coming that by April 1st I would have baskets in the mudroom packed and ready for the beach. New towels would be folded up with some fun beach toys and a bag of snacks. My husband used to laugh at me but when that first nice day came I was ready. The baskets would go in the car and I would pick the girls up from school and go right to the lake for a swim. Everything was packed and ready to go and we always had fun. It's great to be spontaneous, and when you are ready and set up for it, it goes smoothly.

I had four brothers and my mother used to say they needed to run laps around the house several times after school. She realized that sitting in school all day had to be balanced not by screen time but by simply going outdoors and playing. Fun time, running time, biking time. As my dog trainer says, "a tired dog is a good dog." Same goes with kids. How are you balancing the day? What is the rhythm of your day and your week. Have you planned tech-free time, nature time, relaxation to balance out the stress that kids feel living in a city or having an intense school day?

Balance is the key result of planning. When we lived in New York City I would pick my kids up from school with our golden retriever Kasey and head over to Central Park where we would spend time sitting in the grass climbing the Alice in Wonderland statue and having some downtime in nature. Living in a city means having lots of wonderful things, but more stress as well. I always had to plan extra time in nature to balance out the general stress that existed in just everyday life. Going from the high level of noise and sheer amount of stimulation that their city day has to technology filled afternoon was too much. I love technology but this is not away to relax, connect with your heart and feel joyful (one of my goals/intentions of a mindful home). So I invite you to think about and plan ahead to have a balanced day.

positive feelings

Everything is energy, what we put out comes back to us. Isn't it easier to just be positive? I don't see the glass half full, I see it overflowing. We have the power to view and see things in a positive way. What we focus on grows, so why not focus on the good in everybody in the home? Focus on the good in your spouse, your pet, your kids and they will do the same for you. It's a win-win situation. Make a playlist of happy songs and play it every morning. How easy is this...and guess what? It fills the house with happy words and happy energy. A mindful home has a vibration

Positive thoughts generate positive feelings and generate positive life

of joy in it and this is one of the easiest ways to do it. Your kids will be singing those songs all day and sending out happy vibes to those they meet. Say positive things to your child. We all know how good it feels to have a friend that loves and appreciates you just the way you are. We can feel it when we are around them. Do the same for your child; let them know positive qualities about them that you appreciate. Better yet, write them down. Put them on a sticky note in their backpack, on their bathroom mirror or somewhere where they will see and feel the positive message. Or write just a general positive message.

My grandmother used to say to me that I could be anything I wanted to be. Know what? I believed her, and even now when I am going after a new dream of mine I repeat a lot "I can be anything I want to be" Those positive words were so powerful to me. How are you positive every day? What positive messages can you send to your kids? What one line can you say to them that might change their lives years later?

My mom used to say, "someday we will look back on this and laugh." I have used that a million times with my kids and it works. Perspective is the key. Thanks Mom for those positive words. She used to sing "Oh what a beautiful morning, oh what a beautiful day." every morning and she had seven children! When she sang that in the morning she was setting up a positive vibe that would last a lifetime. I still sing that song today. So take a moment to focus on the positive aspects of your child and watch them blossom. Every time you say and feel something positive you are, just like watering a plant, helping your child grow into a positive person that knows you believe in them.

la   la   la la   la   la   la

rituals

I have to admit, rituals are my favorite things and some of the easiest ways to have mindfulness be a part of your home. As a mom, I was all about rituals. When you build something into the routine of the day and do them consistently they become very powerful. What are some of the rituals threat you would like to incorporate in your day? Week? Write them down: Write something positive, say something I am grateful for, meditate five minutes, take a walk, write in a journal, spend half an hour in nature, take a deep breath, do five sun salutations... These were just some of mine.

Write them on pieces of paper and, like a puzzle, decide where they will go in your day: Morning, afternoon, night, only on weekends. Wherever you

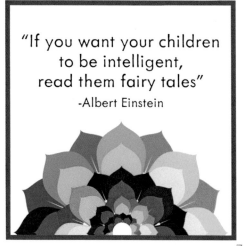

"If you want your children to be intelligent, read them fairy tales"
-Albert Einstein

can fit them in on a regular basis. I am a morning person, so most of mine were in the morning. Every morning I got up, walked the dog, then I wrote in my journal and the day was set up to win. Both walking in the woods and writing became a source where I could channel messages. Even now if I don't do these things I can't write or think straight. Then I lit incense and did five sun salutations and all was well in my world. This wasn't hard and did not take much time. Place the puzzle pieces where you think they go and move them around until you have found the perfect fit for you. Keep it simple and then start doing it consistently. You will be amazed what will happen.

practice non-judgment

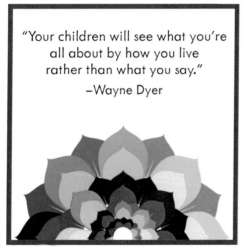

"Your children will see what you're all about by how you live rather than what you say."
–Wayne Dyer

Now we are getting into the hard stuff. But this one is worth it. We all know the feeling of being around someone who is critical of anther human being. Unfortunately this is often true with moms talking and judging other moms. Moms that work judge moms that don't work and vice versa. We all know the feeling when someone is judging another and we wonder what he or she says about us. We have all had that feeling and it doesn't feel good. Judgment gets you nowhere. What is bullying but aggressive judgment of others? Everyone is faced with their own challenges. Until you have walked in someone's shoes it is unfair to judge. This is the opposite of gratitude and positive thinking. Judgment creates a negative energy and doesn't benefit anyone.

My daughter Kayle was born being non-judgmental. She always sees the best in everyone and refuses to talk badly about people. It is no surprise that she ended up in journalism. Seeing both sides to every story gives her the perfect foundation for storytelling. My brother Tommy is the same way. As the oldest of seven siblings, his model of non-judgment provided a strong foundation for the rest of us. It is a very subtle vibration, unlike gratitude which is very strong. But although it is subtle non-judgment is a powerful thing to model for your children.

feel your feelings

Negative feelings are just as powerful as positive ones. When they are bottled up inside or pushed down they become more powerful and even get controlling. Everyone can feel when you walk into a home and the vibration is anger. You can feel it in the pit of your stomach and it doesn't feel good at all. It is important to be able to feel negative feelings and express them in a healthy way in order to move past them. When people spend lifetimes pushing down feelings they get depressed, or worse.

"Just when the caterpillar thought the world was over, it become a butterfly."
–Proverb

Picture a wave. When you start to feel sad or angry visualize a wave coming over your body. Some waves of emotions can feel like tidal waves and others like a rip current. It never feels good. Sometimes they creep up on you in the middle of the night and they can be scary. Trust me, if you feel them just like a wave they will come on strong but go out and produce a softness. In my book **The Bright Blue Balloon** I talk about putting the feeling in a balloon and letting them go. Writing them down helps to clarify feelings. This is a great activity to do with children. Draw a balloon and write down what the feelings are and name the feeling. I feel sad, angry, whatever, when this happens to me. Then picture the balloon flying off. Sometimes we would write them on a piece of paper and burn them in the fireplace or in a campfire at the beach. Being mindful is not just about joy and love. The only way to real joy is through experiences and feeling **all** your feelings.

gratitude

I saved the best for last. I cannot, cannot, CANNOT emphasize this one enough! This is the string that ties everything in a nice tight little bow. This is the key to a joyful life. And guess what? It is just a habit. Get up, brush your teeth and feel grateful every day! Just like playing happy music every day, an attitude of gratitude becomes the voice that plays inside your head. Be grateful for your day, for your kids, for your neighborhood, for the sun, for the stars, for your pet, spouse, friends, health, food and anything else you can think of. That good vibration will go out and more things that you can be grateful for will show up. It's a real win-win situation for everyone involved. Your friends will feel it, your kids will absorb it, and the world will be a better place.

Can you imagine if our news stations showed gratitude each evening? I often imagine how different the world would be if instead of focusing relentlessly on disasters, they began and ended each newscast with gratitude. The world would be a better place.

What I like about gratitude is that it's easy. The more you do it the easier it is. Gratitude journals can help us all, especially children, focus on the good. We had journals that my daughters wrote in or drew pictures in each night. Going to bed with positive thoughts and a heart filled with gratitude set up their evening for a restful sleep. I loved saying one thing about my children each night that I was grateful for and they said one thing back to me. If you can only incorporate one thing in the book please make it gratitude. It really is the key to a peaceful heart and a joyful life.

The secret to happiness
is gratitude

Here is your daily guide of simple steps towards a peaceful home. This workbook offers many different strategies for you to try. My intention is for you to find the ones you like and incorporate those on a consistent basis.

Each day, reflect on how it feels to do the activity together. You will find space to write your reflections down each day. Here are some great starting points to consider:

- **How did you child respond?**
- *Did it feel natural to you?*
- **How did it add to your day?**

day 1 | Send love from your heart to their hearts

As you wake up in the morning, before you get out of bed, take a moment to breathe and connect to your heart. Focus on your children and picture their hearts. Send love, light and energy from your heart to theirs and back again to you. The more you love, the more love comes to you. And I promise you, they will feel it. I still do this with my children, who are in their twenties and live across the country.

reflections

_____

_____

_____

_____

_____

_____

_____

_____

_____

_____

_____

_____

_____

_____

_____

day 2 | Focus on what you are grateful for in your child

What you focus on grows. (Hint: This works on husbands too.) Practice, during the day, saying the words out loud and even writing them down.

Example for a headstrong, precocious child: "I am grateful that my child listens to her inner voice and can make her own decisions."

reflections

_____
_____
_____
_____
_____
_____
_____
_____
_____
_____
_____
_____
_____

day 3 | Make homemade play dough and pound out emotions

Find a great recipe for homemade play dough online (there are dozens). This is fun for all ages, even parents. You can be as creative as you like by making different shapes, creatures or flowers. I always loved pounding out my feelings and anger into the dough by kneading it just like dough. Teach your child that pounding the dough is a great way to express anger and usually ends in laughter.

reflections

_____

_____

_____

_____

_____

_____

_____

_____

_____

_____

_____

_____

_____

_____

_____

day 4 | Make gratitude journals

You can buy a journal and decorate it or make one out of paper. See my instructions on page 45.

The very intention of making a gratitude journal is positive. Focusing on the good things in life will only bring more good things.

reflections

_____

_____

_____

_____

_____

_____

_____

_____

_____

_____

_____

_____

_____

_____

_____

_____

day 5 | Remember to breathe

It is so important to remember to breathe deeply throughout day. Give yourself a moment to relax. Breathing is life-saving in stressful situations. When you're feeling overwhelmed (and who isn't), stressed out or angry, take three deep breaths. These deep breaths will help calm and center you, helping you deal with any situation.

reflections

_____

_____

_____

_____

_____

_____

_____

_____

_____

_____

_____

_____

_____

_____

_____

day 6 | Put sticky notes in their lunch or backpack

Can you imagine the feeling of receiving a note from your parents as a child? "I am so grateful for you because…" "You're perfect because…" "I love you because…"

Words are powerful and this only takes a few moments and can create a lifetime of memories. If you put the note in your child's lunchbox, it will be sweeter than any type of dessert.

Kids not in school yet, or home-schooled? How about "hiding" the note on a bathroom mirror or by a light switch? It's like finding a secret message; your children will love it.

reflections

_____

_____

_____

_____

_____

_____

_____

_____

_____

_____

_____

_____

_____

_____

day 7 | Create an intention board and hang it where everyone can see it

Here's the idea: "In this house, we…" Write down the things that matter to you and your family. "In this house, we are kind to living creatures." "We live in our hearts and let our intuition guide us." I've seen these framed and I've also seen them painted on walls. Intention sets everything else in motion. Seeing it written down on a wall every day is extremely powerful.

reflections

_____

_____

_____

_____

_____

_____

_____

_____

_____

_____

_____

_____

_____

_____

day 8 | Be kind and compassionate to animals

Recently, I visited my adult daughter in New York City. What did she want to do? Visit the farm rescue in upstate New York.

Take your dog on a special walk with your children and focus about the dog...Feed ducks at the pond.

Make an effort to do something nice for a living creature.

reflections

_____

_____

_____

_____

_____

_____

_____

_____

_____

_____

_____

_____

_____

_____

day 9 | Take a tech-free walk

It doesn't matter if it's five minutes or fifty minutes. Go outside and take a simple walk, hike, stroll through the grass. Be mindful of what's around you - notice the birds in trees and the beautiful trees and flowers along the path. Point them out to your child. Be in the moment and enjoy nature. Bring some things back for your nature table (see page 44).

reflections

_____

_____

_____

_____

_____

_____

_____

_____

_____

_____

_____

_____

_____

_____

day 10 | Bake bread

Besides the fact that it smells so good, it is a really fun way to engage your child in cooking and baking. Get a simple recipe, pound and knead, laugh and create delicious bread. And the best part is eating it hot out of the oven with lots of butter.

reflections

_____

_____

_____

_____

_____

_____

_____

_____

_____

_____

_____

_____

_____

_____

_____

_____

_____

day 11 | Make vegetable soup together

It's always a good idea to include children in the chopping and creating of food. Children love to help with meal time. With vegetable soup, you can't really go wrong. Let them pick the vegetables they want in the soup. Grab some cutting board and knives (sharp or butter knife depending on the age) and have them cut and chop to their heart's content.

reflections

_____

_____

_____

_____

_____

_____

_____

_____

_____

_____

_____

_____

_____

_____

day 12 | Play a game that you loved as a child, together

Sharing your favorite game from your childhood allows your child to see that you were a kid once also. You might play games like tic-tac-toe, hopscotch, board games, twister, kick the can, or card games.

Tell them some stories you associate with the games and how they made you feel.

reflections

_____

_____

_____

_____

_____

_____

_____

_____

_____

_____

_____

_____

_____

_____

_____

_____

day 13 | Make a playlist of happy songs to play every morning and fill the house with happiness

What music makes you smile? It could be a song you liked as child like "You Are my Sunshine" or something contemporary that makes you want to groove. Music elicits lots of emotions - make them joyful ones! Extra credit if you dance around with them!

reflections

_____

_____

_____

_____

_____

_____

_____

_____

_____

_____

_____

_____

_____

_____

_____

_____

day 14 | Say the words out loud: "I am grateful for..."

Remember all of those wonderful, grateful thoughts that you had about your child? Now, it's time to tell them.

reflections

_____

_____

_____

_____

_____

_____

_____

_____

_____

_____

_____

_____

_____

_____

_____

_____

day 15 | Salute the Sun

Start your morning quietly and do 3 Sun Salutations before the craziness of life takes over.

Adding three Sun Salutations is a way to incorporate yoga stretches that create a flexible body and spirit. They warm you up like the sun.

See page 46 for instructions.

reflections

_____

_____

_____

_____

_____

_____

_____

_____

_____

_____

_____

_____

_____

_____

day 16 | Take a relaxation journey together

Instead of reading your child a story tonight, take a relaxation journey as your child drifts to sleep. Take a walk on the beach, go for a hike in the forest. Point out all of the things you see and let your child's imagination take it from there. I have a guide of one of the meditation journeys that I take kids on at page 45.

reflections

_____

_____

_____

_____

_____

_____

_____

_____

_____

_____

_____

_____

_____

_____

_____

_____

_____

day 17 | Countdown & Meditate before bed

Do a countdown meditation before bed. While they're lying in bed, tell them to breathe, relax, and let go as you count down from ten to one.

reflections

_____

_____

_____

_____

_____

_____

_____

_____

_____

_____

_____

_____

_____

_____

_____

_____

_____

_____

day 18 | Plant seeds

Plant seeds in a window garden or planter. Teach your child to water and care for the plants as they blossom and grow.

reflections

_____

_____

_____

_____

_____

_____

_____

_____

_____

_____

_____

_____

_____

_____

_____

_____

_____

_____

_____

day 19 | Laugh & be silly

Yes, it seems silly to make an effort to remember to laugh, but it's important to let go sometimes. Take a moment with your child and just be as goofy as you can be. Soak in the giggles from them and don't forget to laugh yourself!

reflections

_____

_____

_____

_____

_____

_____

_____

_____

_____

_____

_____

_____

_____

_____

_____

_____

day 20 | Visualize a rainbow of light

Practice letting go of fear and worry by wrapping your child in a rainbow of light. Often times, parents are worried about their kids for various reasons. Instead of worrying, send them positive energy by closing your eyes, picturing your child and wrapping them in a blanket of rainbow light.

reflections

day 21 | Go on a mindful walk with a basket and pick up objects for your nature table

This is fun to do at the change of seasons. Find acorns, leaves, interesting sticks or anything that is native to where you live. Fill the basket and make your nature table come alive!

See instructions on page 44.

reflections

_____

_____

_____

_____

_____

_____

_____

_____

_____

_____

_____

_____

_____

_____

_____

_____

day 22 | Play outside!

Leave the dishes in the sink and take the kids out to play. Just have fun! Extra points if you leave your phone at home!

reflections

_____

_____

_____

_____

_____

_____

_____

_____

_____

_____

_____

_____

_____

_____

_____

_____

_____

_____

_____

day 23 | Have a family movie night

Enjoy family movie night with a positive film that makes you feel good. Gather some fun snacks, popcorn, fruit, cheese and crackers and snuggle up all together to watch.

This is a great opportunity to watch a movie from your childhood, share memories that you have of that film with your child. One of my favorites is **Mary Poppins**.

reflections

_____

_____

_____

_____

_____

_____

_____

_____

_____

_____

_____

_____

_____

_____

_____

_____

day 24 | Read your favorite book from your childhood

Share memories that you have with this book: How old you were when you read it, how it made you feel, why it was important to you. My favorite was always **The Little Engine that Could.**

reflections

_____

_____

_____

_____

_____

_____

_____

_____

_____

_____

_____

_____

_____

_____

_____

_____

_____

day 25 | Make a collage

Get scissors, photos, glue sticks and markers. Use the collages to illustrate happy memories or moments. The act of creating the collages not only reinforces the happy memories, but it itself will become one. Display the collages, or even laminate them and use them as place mats!

reflections

_____

_____

_____

_____

_____

_____

_____

_____

_____

_____

_____

_____

_____

_____

_____

_____

_____

_____

day 26 | Balloon feelings

Children (and adults!) can sometimes have a hard time expressing their feelings, especially negative ones. Draw a balloon and inside the balloon, help them draw and/or write their feelings: "I am frustrated/sad/angry when..." Practice closing your eyes and imagining the balloon floating off to the sky. You'll be amazed at how good this feels.

reflections

day 27 | Positive thinking exercise

Spend a moment with your child and quiet your mind. Have them close their eyes and imagine a beautiful day. Ask them what color do they see and what do they feel. Tell them to focus on that color and ask them to remember that positive feeling several times throughout the day.

reflections

_____

_____

_____

_____

_____

_____

_____

_____

_____

_____

_____

_____

_____

_____

_____

_____

day 28 | Go stargazing

Take a walk outside at night. Look up at the stars and feel how big the world really is. Ask your child, "How does it make you feel when you look up at the stars?"

reflections

_____

_____

_____

_____

_____

_____

_____

_____

_____

_____

_____

_____

_____

_____

_____

_____

day 29 | Reflect on your day

Encourage the child to say three things that he or she was grateful that day.

reflections

_____

_____

_____

_____

_____

_____

_____

_____

_____

_____

_____

_____

_____

_____

_____

_____

_____

_____

_____

day 30 | Echoing gratitude

Express to your child what about them you're grateful for and have them do the same for you. What goes around comes around.

reflections

_____

_____

_____

_____

_____

_____

_____

_____

_____

_____

_____

_____

_____

_____

_____

closing

Trying to incorporate and maintain 30 new things into your household routine is almost impossible, and I get it! To me, it is more important to take 3 or 4 activities and do them consistently, than all 30 every once in a while. This book is intended to be a guide to help you find the methods and activities that work **best** in your home. Remember these words from the Buddha: ***"There is no path to happiness - happiness is the path."*** Be open to trying new things and take note of what works and what doesn't - and why. Also know that this book isn't going anywhere and you can come back to different activities as your family grows and changes.

These are the four things that I was able to incorporate in a consistent basis into my children's lives. This is an opportunity to show your children that what you focus on grows. Any moment that you have together, without technology interrupting the flow, will allow all of you to connect with each other and with joy.

Making a Nature Table

- Find a small table area, preferably one that you see often in a hallway or near the front door
- Put a pretty cloth on it and find a sweet vase for flowers
- Go outside and take a nature walk with your child with a basket or bag
- Find some pretty wildflowers, twigs, leaves, acorns, rocks, bark, moss, birds nests, or anything that you like
- Arrange your findings on the table. It's nice to add fresh flowers, crystals, a book of poems.

You may write out a pretty saying and lean it against the vase or add a candle. This beautiful table brings the energy of nature indoors, shows gratitude and appreciation for the earth. It reflects the beautiful season that nature provides.

Meditation Journey

As your children is lying down to go to sleep, have them close their eyes and relax all the parts of their bodies. With three deep breaths, each exhale relaxes more into the bed. Pick a nature spot that you would like to go to, like the ocean or the forest. Start to talk about going to that place. Point out the sights, sounds, and smells that you encounter on your mindful journey. Ensure you touch on every sense. Count down from five to one, as you encourage them to go deeper and deeper into a place of peace.

Example:

I am lying on the soft, deep sand. I feel my body relax into the earth as the sun pours warmth, light and energy all through my body. I hear the sound of the surf washing along the shore, in and out, as my entire body relaxes even more...

Gratitude Journal

- Buy some fun, colorful paper for the cover of the journal. Find some more neutral colors for the inside pages.
- Punch holes in the sides of the paper and use yarn to bind the papers together
- Decorate the cover with images, leaves, nature objects, pictures. Anything to make it yours. Add the year.
- Have your child write in it every night. If your child can't write yet, let her draw and then write in the words that she tells you.

Sun Salutation

Adding three sun salutations is a way to incorporate yoga stretches that create a flexible body and spirit. They warm you up like the sun.

- Reach your arms towards the sky
- Swan dive forward, bring your arms down, folding at the hips
- Flat back (look at me and smile!)
- Bend both knees so your hands are on the ground and step foot back, so you're in the shape of a lunge
- Arms come around the front foot, step the other foot back, plank pose!
- Knees, chest and chin come to the ground, cobra (kiss the floor + slither)
- Come onto your hands and knees, then downward dog (wag your tail)
- Step forward. Forward fold.
- Slowly roll up to standing, reach your hands up to the sky
- Bring your hands to your heart

crafts & activities

Crafts are a way to create wonderful and mindful moments with your kids. Here are some of my favorite things. Discover even more on Pinterest.

- Homemade play dough
- Tissue paper butterflies
- Creative food art (making a sunflower out of pancakes and orange slices)
- Tic-tac-toe outside with chalk
- Painted branches
- Firefly jars
- Spray chalk recipe
- Making vegetable soup together
- Life-size portraits (don't forget to write all the wonderful qualities they like about themselves)
- Prayer flags
- Tie-dyed shirts

praise for
Raising Peaceful Kids

"This parenting guide weaves Ms. Walsh's professional and personal experiences as a teacher and parent making for an engaging read. Full of practical tips for teaching children to be aware of their world, use their imaginations and feel peaceful."

~ Kristin Bundesen, Ph.D, educator

"[This book] is a life-long model created by Kathy Walsh, who has over 20 years' experience in education and gives parents the tools needed to raise children in a mindful and compassionate way. Each chapter is filled with illustrations and simple examples for children to follow...By building good character now, parents can mold the headlines of the future by teaching kids today (and every day) how to value peace."

~ Beauty News NYC

"To raise peaceful kids, promote peace at home. It's a simple concept but not always easy to carry through. In *Raising Peaceful Kids,* author Kathy Walsh produces a conversational guide to get parents thinking about how their actions and reactions shape their kids' lives."

~ Betsy, blogger on OVParent

Those who know Kathy's story will tell you that her career and position as a mindfulness expert is no coincidence. Inspired by her whimsical and influential childhood experiences, Kathy set out to live a positive life of mindfulness and peace. A master meditator and avid reader and author of mindfulness books, Kathy created a series of children's books and meditations called Joyohboy. Boasting more than 20 years of experience working with children, the arts, and education, Kathy finds nothing more exciting than helping children and their families find a life of joy. Kathy created Peace Place for Kids to help children connect to peace through mindfulness, meditation and movement. Kathy teaches workshops and classes for kids and speaks at conferences and events to parents and early childhood professionals about raising peaceful kids.

She has two beautiful daughters, Kara and Kayle and they have four peaceful rescue pups, Maddie, Coco, Bruce and Stella. She co-owns a mindful marketing company, KnockKnock Social with her business partner Meredith and her two rescue pups, Barnaby and Samson.

Kathy has been featured on National press, radio, blog sites and TV. She was interviewed on a segment on NPR Los Angeles, is a regular blogger on Huffington Post and has been featured on Elephant Journal.

The Joyohboy book series is part of
Peace Place for Kids

It's not about finding peace or looking for peace. It's about connecting with peace. At Peace Place, we give children the tools to connect with the place of peace. You can't strive, work hard, or study hard to find peace. Peace is a place of letting go and then the connection happens. How do children who are taught the opposite learn to let go? We let go of tension in the body through movement and exercises that move energy. We let go of thought through medita-tion. We let go of control by focusing on positive energy filled with gratitude. Why peace? Because peace is where your life soars.

Connecting with peace puts the child in harmony with life. When children connect with peace, they live a life of joy, because that is what they attract. They are able to go to that place of peace inside, no matter what is happening on the outside, and ultimately, peace is where the power lies. They are in control when they are at peace. External influences don't bother them. When children connect with peace, they are able to listen to their own inner voice and intuition. Intuition guides the children to do what is best for them, which brings them to a vibration of peace. This vibration of peace attracts more good things and takes the child round and round in a circle of joy. Join us on this mindful journey raising peaceful kids in a vibration of love.

peace place
for kids*

facebook.com/joyohboybooks f 🐦 twitter.com/peaceplace4kids
instagram.com/peaceplaceforkids 📷 ⓟ pinterest.com/peaceplace4kids

www.peaceplaceforkids.com

Made in the USA
Las Vegas, NV
05 January 2021